USBORNE SPOTTER'S STICKER BOOKS
HORSES
AND PONIES

Joanna Spector

Designed by Terry Shannon

Illustrated by Sue Testar, David Wright, Elaine Keenan and Malcolm McGregor

Cover design by Candice Whatmore
Cover photograph by Tom Nebbia/CORBIS
Series editor: Jane Chisholm

How to use this book

There are over sixty different horses in this book. Using the descriptions and the line drawings, try to match each sticker with the right horse. If you need help, there is a list at the back of the book that tells you which sticker goes with which horse. You can also use this book as a spotter's handbook to make a note of which horses you have seen.

Here are some of the words used to describe parts of a horse.

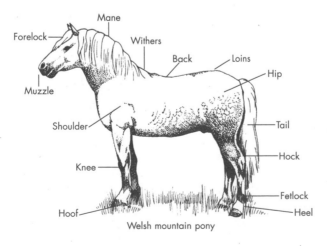

Mane
Forelock
Withers
Back
Loins
Hip
Muzzle
Shoulder
Tail
Hock
Knee
Fetlock
Hoof
Heel

Welsh mountain pony

PONIES

Ponies are fourteen hands and two inches high, or under. This height is measured from the ground to the bottom of the pony's neck (its withers).

A few ponies still live wild in herds, on moors and in forests or hilly places. But most of them have been tamed, and are now kept as riding ponies or pets.

◁ Exmoor
Height: up to 12.3 hands

Place	
Date	

This hardy, strong-willed pony is the oldest breed in Britain, and still lives half wild in herds on Exmoor. It is always brown or bay, with a light belly and nose. It is a very popular riding pony for children.

Dartmoor ▷
Height: up to 12.2 hands

Place	
Date	

This tough little British pony roams half wild on Dartmoor. It is intelligent and sure-footed, and makes a good children's riding pony. Its coat may be bay, black or brown. Look out for its small, pretty head.

◁ **Fell**

Height: about 14 hands

Place	
Date	

This large, sturdy pony comes from the Pennine hills in Britain, and is still used by farmers for herding sheep and cattle. It is usually black, but it can also be brown or bay. It never has any white markings.

Highland ▷

Height: up to 14.2 hands

Place	
Date	

This large trekking pony comes from the highlands of Scotland. It is usually grey or dun, but can also be black or chestnut. It grows a long coat in winter. Look out for its thick mane and tail.

◁ **Shetland**

Height: about 9.2 hands

Place	
Date	

This strong little pony comes from the Shetland Islands in Britain and is a popular pet. Its rough coat is usually brown, black or chestnut, but it can also be piebald or skewbald. Look out for its short neck.

PONIES

Welsh mountain ▷

Height: up to 12 hands

Place	
Date	

This old breed comes from Wales and is a popular pony for riding and driving. It has Arab and thoroughbred blood, which gives it an elegant head. Its coat can be any shade, except piebald or skewbald.

◁ Camargue

Height: up to14.2 hands

Place	
Date	

This ancient breed comes from swampland at the mouth of the River Rhone in France, and is very strong and tough. Some ponies are used to herd cattle, but many of them still live wild in herds.

Connemara ▷

Height: 13-14.2 hands

Place	
Date	

This attractive pony comes from northwest Ireland, and was probably first bred from Spanish and Arab horses. It is fast and sure-footed. Its coat is usually grey, but can also be dun, black, brown, bay or chestnut.

Gotland/Russ ▷

Height: about 12.2 hands

Place	
Date	

This ancient breed has lived on the Swedish island of Gotland since the Stone Age. It is a very good trotter and jumper. Its coat can be any shade, but is usually brown, bay or chestnut.

◁ Haflinger

Height: about 14 hands

Place	
Date	

This pretty, sure-footed pony comes from Austria. It is used in forestry work, to pull and carry loads up hills. It is also ridden and driven in harness. Look out for its chestnut coat and flaxen mane and tail.

Fjord ▷

Height: 13-14.2 hands

Place	
Date	

This strong pony comes from Norway. It is used for all types of work, such as riding, driving, hauling and carrying. Look out for its yellow dun coat, and its black and silver mane which is cut in the shape of a crest.

PONIES

◁ Caspian

Height: 9.2-11.2 hands

Place	
Date	

This small, dainty pony comes from Iran. It looks like a tiny thoroughbred horse with its long legs, and is very good at jumping. Its coat is usually bay, brown or grey and never has any white markings.

Przewalski ▷

Height: 12-14 hands

Place	
Date	

This tough breed is also called the Asiatic or Mongolian wild horse, and has not changed since the Ice Age. Only a few exist, and are mostly kept in zoos. It is bay or dun, with a big head and stubby mane.

◁ Sable Island pony

Height: about 14 hands

Place	
Date	

This small pony comes from Nova Scotia in Canada. Its coat is usually chestnut, but can be any shade. It still lives in wild herds and feeds off scrub grass on sand dunes. Tame ones are used as children's riding ponies.

Falabella ◁

Height: less than 7 hands

Place	
Date	

This tiny little pony comes from Argentina. It is not very strong, but it is good-natured and makes a popular pet and driving pony. It has a long, silky coat which can be any shade.

Criollo ▷

Height: 14 hands and over

Place	
Date	

This big pony comes from South America, and is descended from Barb, Andalusian and other Spanish horses. It is a good jumper and is used to play polo. Its coat is dun, roan, brown, skewbald, black or bay.

Pony of the Americas (POA) ◁

Height: 11.2-13.2 hands

Place	
Date	

This pony is a modern breed from the USA, and makes a good children's riding pony. Its coat has a spotted pattern, which is similar to the coat of the Appaloosa horse. Look out for its dark muzzle.

RIDING HORSES

Horses are bigger than ponies, and are more than fourteen hands and two inches high. Different types of horses are used for different kinds of work.

Riding horses are fairly light and strong. They are often used for herding cattle, racing, showjumping, dressage, and pulling carriages, as well as for riding.

◁ Thoroughbred

Height: 15-16 hands

Place	
Date	

This elegant horse was originally bred from Arab horses in England. It is very powerful with long legs, and is the fastest horse in the world. Its coat can be any solid shade, such as black, grey, bay or chestnut.

Arab/Arabian ▷

Height: 14.2-15.1 hands

Place	
Date	

This horse first came from the deserts of Arabia and is now bred all over the world. It is often used to race long distances. It is usually brown, chestnut, bay, grey or black, with a small, fine head, an arched neck and a short back.

Quarter horse ▷

Height: 15-16 hands

Place	
Date	

This quick, intelligent horse comes from the USA, and is named after the quarter mile races which it used to run. It is now used on ranches to herd cattle, and for rodeo riding. Its coat can be any shade.

◁ **American saddlebred**

Height: 15-15.3 hands

Place	
Date	

This lively horse was first used as a riding and harness horse in the southern states of the USA. It has three to five ambling gaits which makes it smooth to ride. Its coat is chestnut, brown or bay. See how high it lifts its knees and tail as it trots.

Morgan ▷

Height: 14-15 hands

Place	
Date	

This solid American horse was first bred from a stallion called Justin Morgan, in New England. Its coat can be either chestnut, brown or bay. Look out for its deep, elegant body and thick tail.

Tennessee walking horse ▷

Height: 15-16 hands

Place	
Date	

This horse comes from Tennessee and Louisiana in the USA, and may be any solid shade or roan. It is used for riding, farm work and pulling carriages. It has three special gaits - a slow walk, running walk and "rocking chair" canter.

◁ **Paso fino**

Height: 13-15.2 hands

Place	
Date	

This American show horse is descended from the horses of Spanish explorers, and can be any shade. It has five extra gaits which other horses do not have. Instead of trotting, some do a special slow gait called the "paso fino".

Appaloosa ▷

Height: 14-15.3 hands

Place	
Date	

This horse was once ridden by the Nez Percé Indians of North America. Its coat can be a dark pinkish shade, with a light back and black spots on the loins and hips. It can also be white with black spots, or bay or black with white spots.

Pinto ▷

Height: any height

Place	
Date	

This unusual horse is bred in the USA, and is used for riding and herding. Its patchy coat can have one of two patterns - "overo", with more white patches on the belly, or "tobiano", with more white patches on the back. Most horses can be bred to have pinto markings.

◁ Palomino

Height: any height

Place	
Date	

A palomino horse has a pretty chestnut coat, with a white mane and tail. It is a very popular show horse, but it is also bred to hunt and jump. Most types of ponies and horses can be bred to have palomino coats.

Waler ▷

Height: 15-16 hands

Place	
Date	

This strong horse was first bred in New South Wales in Australia, and can be any shade. It was once used as a cavalry horse, and is now used for riding, showjumping, herding cattle and riding in rodeos.

RIDING HORSES

Akhal-teke ▷

Height: about 15.1 hands

Place	
Date	

This ancient breed comes from Russia, and can bear great heat or cold. It is used for jumping, racing, dressage and trekking. Its fine coat is golden, chestnut, bay, black or brown, with a metallic sheen.

◁ **Don**

Height: 15-16 hands

Place	
Date	

This big horse comes from the Don Valley in Russia, and was once ridden by the Cossacks. It has long legs and a short, jerky stride, and is often used to pull carriages. It is chestnut, beige or grey.

◁ **Turkoman**

Height: 14.3-15.2

Place	
Date	

This sturdy horse is named after its original home in the Turkoman Steppes in northern Iran. It is a good riding horse because it is so strong and tireless. Its coat is usually grey or bay, but can be dun or chestnut.

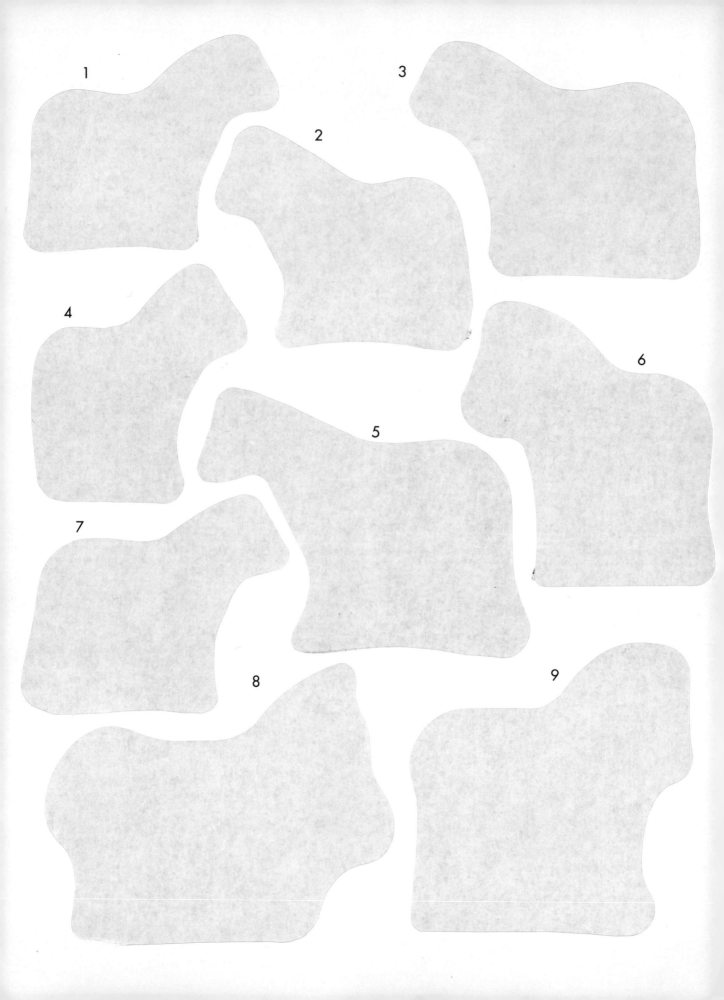

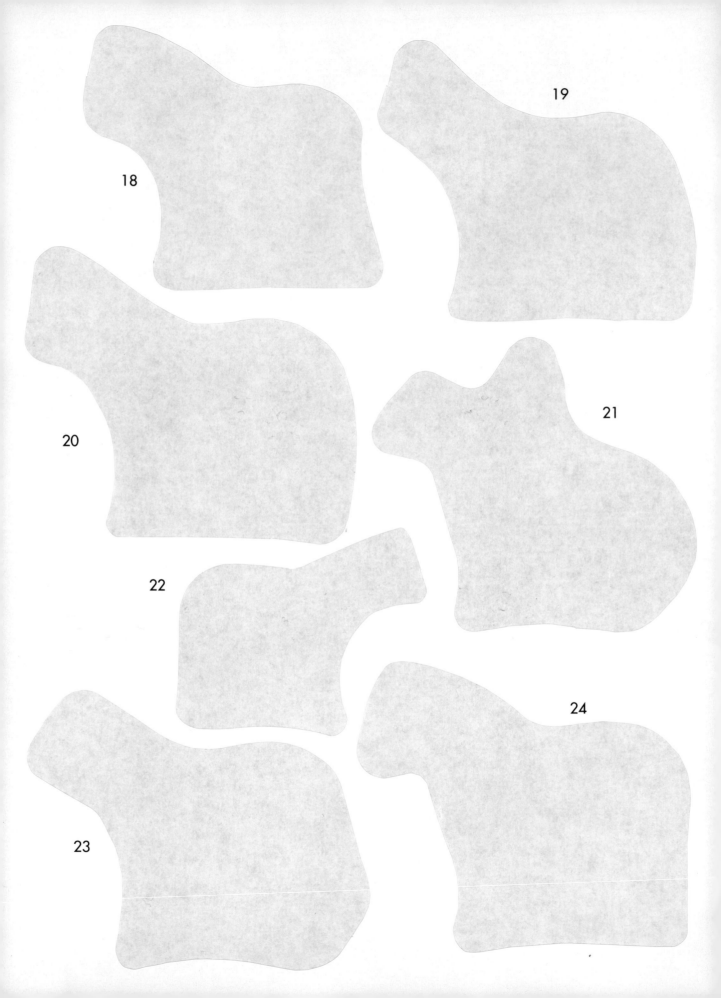

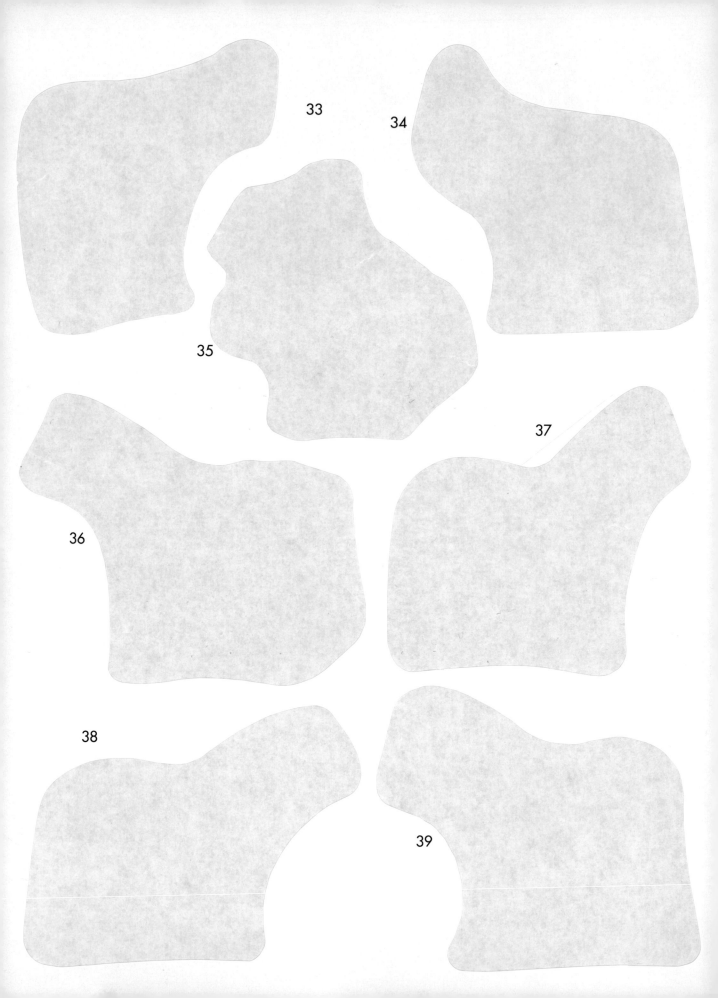

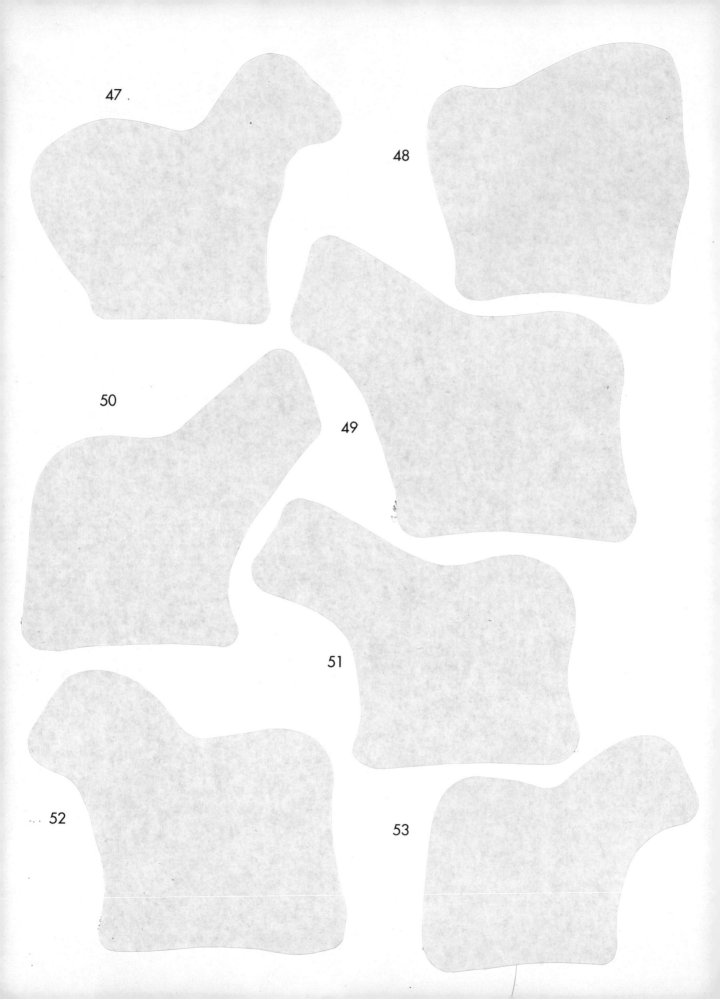

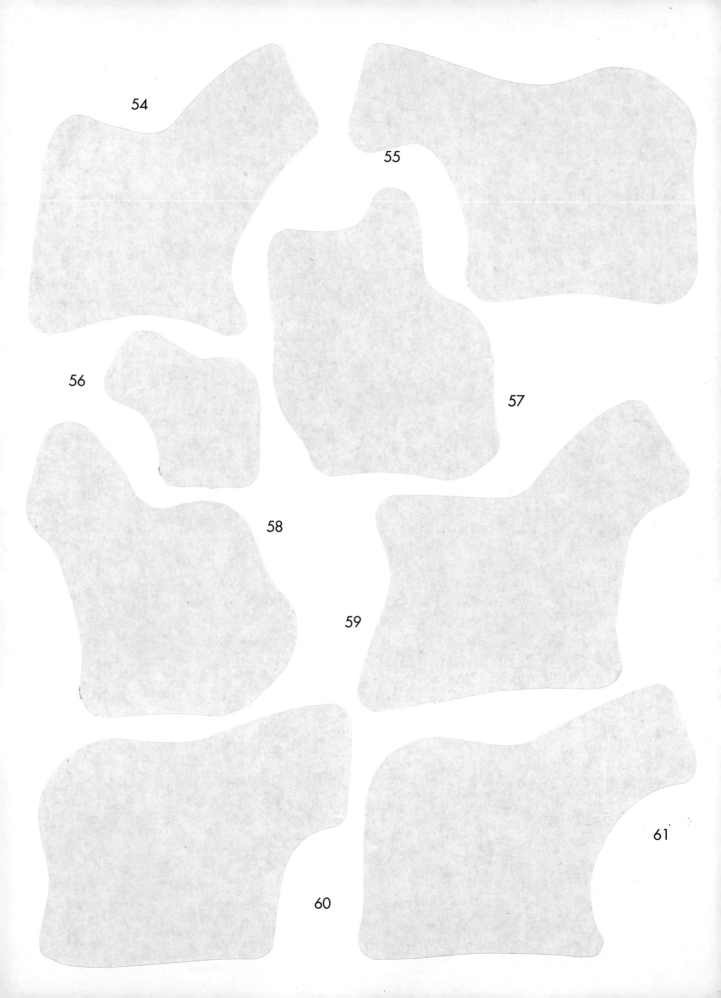

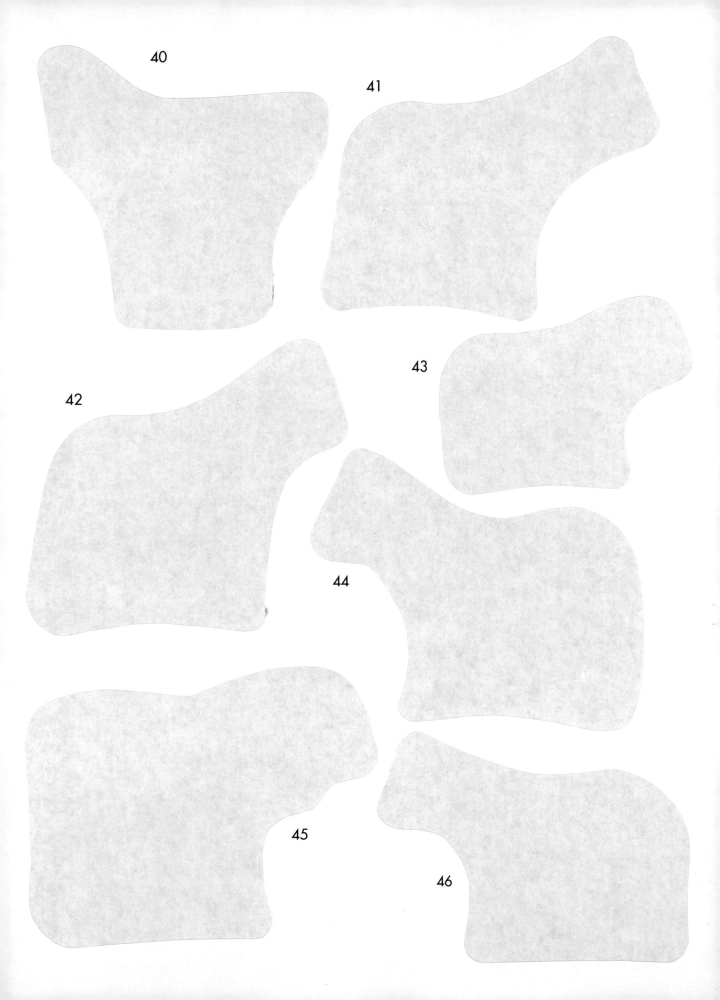

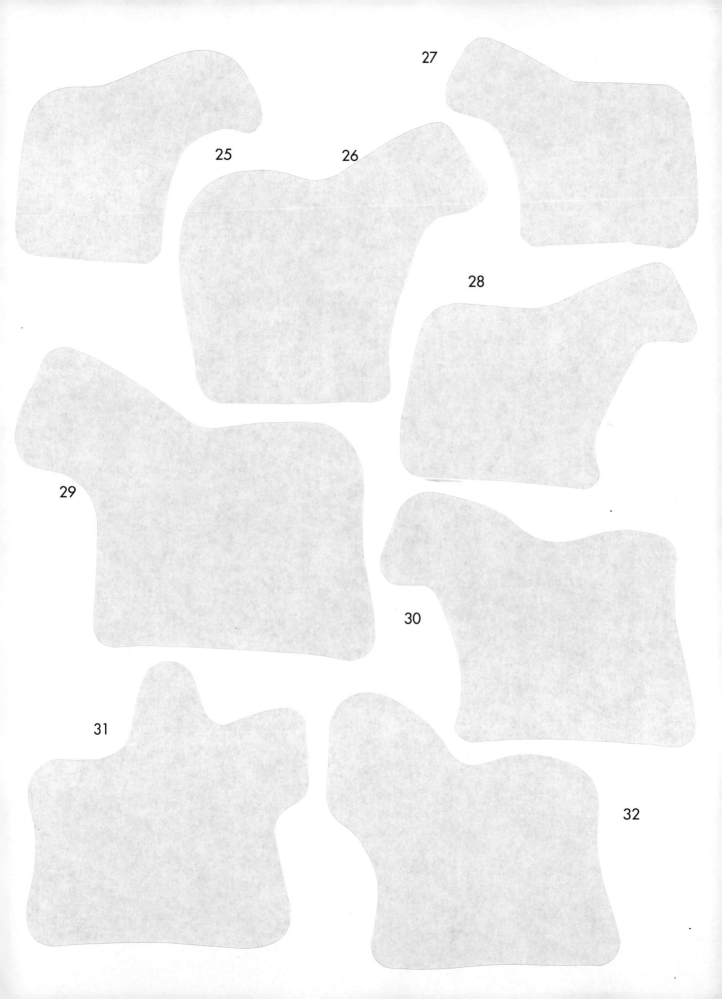

25

26

27

28

29

30

31

32

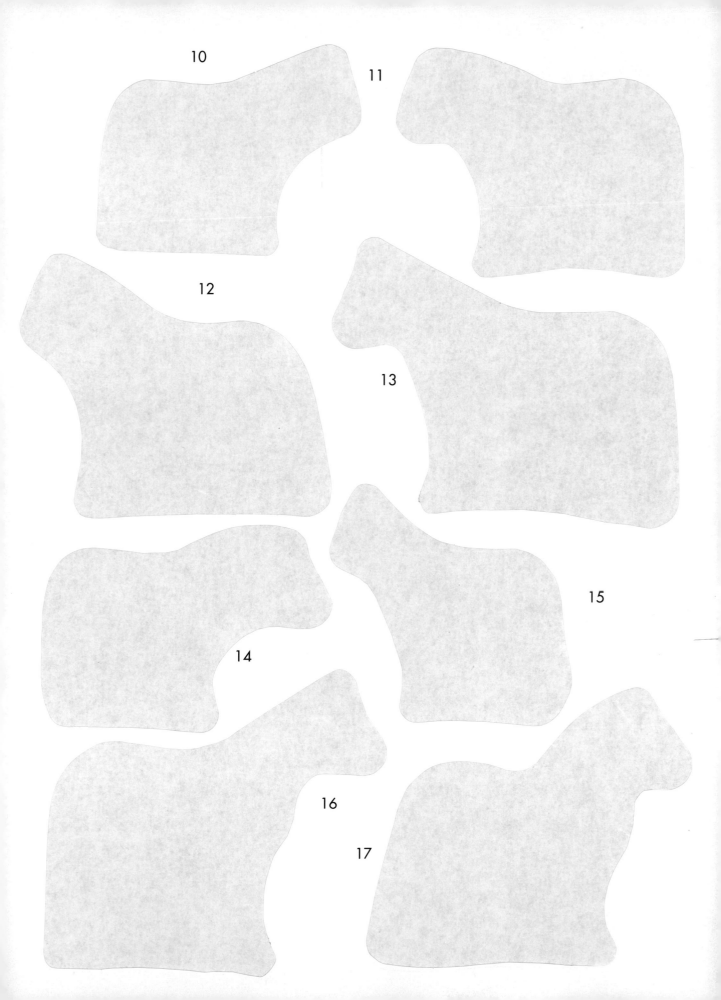

◁ **Andalusian**

Height: 15.2-16 hands

Place	
Date	

This popular Spanish riding horse was first bred from barb and Arab horses and native ponies, and is very sure-footed. Its coat is grey, black, bay or brown. Look out for its arched neck.

Lusitano ▷

Height: 15-16 hands

Place	
Date	

This pretty Portuguese horse has the same ancestry as the Andalusian horse, but is taller and lighter. It is used by the army and on farms. It is also ridden in bullrings, wearing splendid tack. Its coat is grey, brown or bay.

◁ **Barb**

Height: 14-15 hands

Place	
Date	

This small horse comes from North Africa, although there are very few pure-bred barbs left. It has hard legs and feet, and is very fast over short distances. It is usually bay, grey, black, brown or chestnut.

RIDING HORSES

Hanoverian ▷
Height: 16-17 hands

Place	
Date	

This strong German breed is descended from war horses ridden in the Middle Ages. It has powerful hindquarters and heavy shoulders, and makes a good show-jumper. Its coat is often bay or brown, but may be any solid shade.

◁ **Holstein**
Height: 16-16.2 hands

Place	
Date	

This big horse comes from the marshes of the River Elbe in Germany. It makes a good show-jumper and carriage horse, because it is so strong. Its coat is usually brown, bay or black.

Trakehner ▷
Height: 16-16.2 hands

Place	
Date	

This gentle but brave horse is bred mainly in Poland and Germany. It is used as a farm horse and cavalry horse, and is also good at jumping and dressage. Its coat can be bay, brown, chestnut or black. Notice how much its shoulders slope.

Lipizzaner ◁

Height: 14.3-16 hands

Place	
Date	

This famous Austrian horse is used for dressage by the Spanish Riding School in Vienna. It was first bred from Andalusian horses. It is born with a black or brown coat, which later turns grey and then white in old age. Notice its short, arched neck.

Knabstrup ▷

Height: about 15.2 hands

Place	
Date	

This attractive Danish horse is descended from a spotted Spanish mare. It is fast and hardy, and is very popular as a circus horse. Its coat is usually white with black spots.

Døle/Gudbrandsdal ◁

Height: about 15 hands

Place	
Date	

This strong, medium-sized horse is also called an Ostland horse or Dølehest. It comes from Norway, and was once used to pull heavy loads. Its coat is usually brown or bay. Notice its feathered fetlocks.

HARNESS HORSES

Harness horses are stronger and sturdier than riding horses, and are often good trotters. Some harness horses are used to pull carriages on grand occasions.

They are also used to pull carts in some places, in special horse and cart races. Harness horses are also used as working horses on farms, and as riding horses.

◁ **Standardbred**

Height: 15-16 hands

Place	
Date	

This famous harness horse comes from the USA and races in special carts called "sulkies". It is named after the standard speed it needed to reach in order to be registered. Its coat can be any solid shade, but is usually bay, black or brown.

Cleveland Bay ▷

Height: 15-16.2 hands

Place	
Date	

This sure-footed horse comes from Yorkshire in England, and is often used to pull carriages. It is not very fast, but makes a good jumper. Its coat is bay, with no white markings. Notice how much its shoulders slope.

◁ Hackney

Height: 15 hands

Place	
Date	

This lively English horse is famous for its exaggerated but graceful movements, lifting its legs and tail very high as it trots. It is used as a show horse and to pull light carriages. Its coat is bay, black or brown. Notice its long back.

Frederiksborg ▷

Height: up to 16 hands

Place	
Date	

This strong and lively horse is an old breed from Denmark, and has fairly short legs. It is a hard worker, and is often used on farms and as a riding horse. Its coat is chestnut.

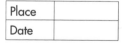

◁ Finnish universal

Height: about 15.2 hands

Place	
Date	

This gentle and alert horse works mainly on farms and in forests in Finland. It is also used in trotting races and for riding. Its coat is usually chestnut, and it often has white markings.

17

HARNESS HORSES

Friesian/Frisian ▷

Height: about 15 hands

Place	
Date	

This strong, good-natured horse is from Friesland in the Netherlands. It was first bred in the Middle Ages to carry knights, and it now works mostly in harness. It is black, with a thick, curly mane and tail, and feathered fetlocks.

◁ Groningen

Height: 15.2-16 hands

Place	
Date	

This sturdy farm horse comes from the Netherlands and can live on very little food. It is heavy but fast, and makes a very good harness or riding horse. Its coat is usually black, bay or brown.

Nonius ▷

Height: 14.2-17 hands

Place	
Date	

This big, strong horse comes from Hungary, where it was first bred from a stallion called Nonius. It is used mainly as a working horse on farms, and its coat is black, bay or brown. It is bred in two sizes - a small breed of 15.2 hands and a large breed of up to 17 hands.

Orlov trotter ▷

Height: 15.2-17 hands

Place	
Date	

This strong, heavy horse comes from Russia, and is named after a Russian called Count Orlov. It lifts its legs fairly high when trotting, and was once used as a cavalry horse. Its coat is often grey, but can be black or bay. Look out for feathering around its fetlocks.

◁ **Wielkopolski**

Height: about 16 hands

Place	
Date	

This popular Polish horse is bred in many sizes, and is usually chestnut, brown or bay. The heavier ones work on farms, and the lighter ones are used to ride or pull carriages. Many are bred at studs owned by the state.

Kladruber ▷

Height: 16-17 hands

Place	
Date	

This black or grey horse comes from the Czech and Slovak republics and was first bred in the 16th century by Emperor Maximilian II. It is used to pull state coaches in teams, and is also seen on farms and in dressage competitions.

HEAVY HORSES

Heavy horses are the largest breeds of horses. They are much bigger and chunkier than riding horses and harness horses, and are also very strong.

They are mainly used to work on farms and to haul heavy loads. In the Middle Ages, many of them were used to carry knights into battle.

◁ **Shire**

Height: up to 18 hands

Place	
Date	

This great English heavy horse once carried knights into battle. It is a hard worker, and is now used as a working horse on farms. Its coat is usually grey, bay or black, with white markings. Look out for its feathered fetlocks.

Suffolk punch ▷

Height: about 16 hands

Place	
Date	

This short, stocky breed is named after its original home in Suffolk in England. It is a very good-natured horse, and can live on very little food. Its coat is always chestnut. Notice its thick neck and wide chest.

Percheron ▷

Height: 15.2-17 hands

Place	
Date	

This popular working horse first came from northern France. It is very strong and often weighs over a ton (tonne), but it only needs a little food. It is also very quiet and easy to handle. Its silky coat can be black or grey.

◁ Breton heavy

Height: 15-16 hands

Place	
Date	

This strong and rugged horse comes from northwest France, and is mainly used as a working horse. Its coat is usually roan, but some Breton heavies can also be bay or chestnut.

Ardennes/Ardennais ▷

Height: about 15.2 hands

Place	
Date	

This ancient breed from France and Belgium was once used by the cavalry of the French emperor, Napoleon. It is strong and gentle, and can live out in bad weather. It is usually chestnut, roan or bay. Notice its heavy neck and shoulders.

HEAVY HORSES

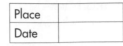 **Pinzgauer noriker**

Height: 15-16 hands

Place	
Date	

This strong, quiet horse is the oldest breed in Austria, and may have been descended from a Roman breed. It is often used as a working horse on farms. Its coat is bay, chestnut or spotted.

Schleswig ▷

Height: 15.2-16 hands

Place	
Date	

This strong, powerful horse comes from northern Germany, and was once used to carry knights into battle. It is now used mostly on farms and for hauling work. Its coat is almost always chestnut.

◁ **Dutch heavy**
Height: 16.3 hands

Place	
Date	

This strong and heavy ancient breed is bred from Belgian horses. It is very popular as a working horse on farms in the Netherlands, where it has its own special show. Its coat is bay, chestnut or grey.

Jutland ▷
Height: 15.2-15.3 hands

Place	
Date	

This strong Danish horse was once used by the Vikings, and has a deep body and short legs. It now works on farms and pulls brewers' wagons in Denmark. It is often chestnut, but can be roan, black, grey, bay or light brown.

◁ **Vladimir**
Height: about 16 hands

Place	
Date	

This strong, active horse is named after its original home in Vladimir in Russia. It is often used for harness work. Its coat can be bay, chestnut or roan. Look out for its high, arched neck.

23

INDEX AND CHECKLIST

This list will help you to find every horse in the book. The first number after each horse's name tells you which page it is on. The second number (in brackets) is the number of its sticker.

GLOSSARY

BAY A light to dark brown horse with black lower legs, mane and tail.

CAVALRY Soldiers on horseback.

CHESTNUT Reddish-brown.

DRESSAGE A method of training horses, often displayed at competitions.

DRIVING HORSE A horse used to pull carts or carriages.

DUN A pale beige horse, with black legs and a dark stripe along its back.

FLAXEN Pale yellow.

GAITS A horse's different paces.

HAND Unit for measuring a horse's height from hoof to withers. Equal to four inches.

PACK PONY A pony used to carry loads.

PIEBALD A black horse with white patches.

POLO A game played on horseback.

ROAN A bay, black or chestnut horse, with white hairs sprinkled on its coat.

RODEO An American horse show at which cowboys display riding and herding skills.

SKEWBALD A horse of any shade, except black, with white patches.

STALLION A male horse used for breeding.

First published in 1994 by Usborne Publishing Ltd., 83-85 Saffron Hill, London EC1N 8RT, England.
Copyright © Usborne Publishing Ltd. 2001, 1997, 1994, 1985, 1978. First published in America, March 1995 UE